WHEN CANAD
THE STORY OF DUTCH

To Sean and Charlie

Albert VanderMey

WHEN CANADA WAS HOME

The Story of Dutch Princess Margriet

A look at the happy events
of 50 years ago that provided
a ray of light, of hope, in
the dark days of
the Second World War.

Foreword by
His Excellency Ramon John Hnatyshyn
Governor General of Canada

Introduction by
His Honour G.W. Baron de Vos van Steenwijk
Ambassador of the Netherlands in Canada

VANDERHEIDE PUBLISHING CO. LTD.
Surrey, B.C. Canada - Lynden, WA, USA

Acknowledgements

Many of the photos used in this book are from the personal files of the author. As usual, Ineke Constantine at the Consulate General of the Netherlands in New York City provided invaluable assistance by offering a generous selection of photos for our consideration. We are grateful also to many individuals and organizations for their fine co-operation during the research for information and photos. It is not our intent to name them all, but we would like to single out the following:

State Institute for War Documentation, Amsterdam
City of Toronto Archives
Martine Feaver, Ottawa
A. van Rijn, Vancouver
Wim van Duyn, Toronto
Royal Netherlands Embassy, Ottawa

National Capital Commission, Ottawa
City of Ottawa Archives
St. Andrew's Presbyterian Church, Ottawa
The Beacon-Herald, Stratford
Imperial War Museum, London
Dr. Paul Puddicombe, Ottawa
National Archives of Canada, Ottawa
State Information Service, The Hague
Legion magazine and editor Mac Johnston
Albert van der Heide, publisher,
the Windmill Herald, Surrey, B.C.

The publishers have attempted to trace the origin of the photographs as much as possible. In case a source has been overlooked, we sincerely apologize for this oversight, and would welcome being informed about it.

WHEN CANADA WAS HOME
The Story of Dutch Princess Margriet

No part of this publication may be reproduced, stored in a retrieval system, or transmitted in any form, or by any means, electronic, mechanical, photocopying, recording or otherwise, without the prior written permission of Vanderheide Publishing Co. Ltd.

ISBN 1-895815-02-9

Printed by Hemlock Printers Ltd.,
Burnaby, B.C., Canada.

Canadian Cataloguing in Publication Data

VanderMey, Albert
When Canada Was Home

ISBN 1-895815-02-9

1. Margriet, Princess of the Netherlands.
1943- 2. Margriet, Princess of the
Netherlands, 1943- --Pictorial works.
3. Netherlands--Princess and princesses--
Biography. I. Title.
DJ289.A4M374 1992 949.207'2'092 092-091834-4

Copyright 1992 Vanderheide Publishing Co. Ltd.

DE ORANJEKRANT

(VIVERE MILITARE EST)

JAARGANG 1943   No. 16

Verschijnt tenminste éénmaal p. maand
GEREDIGEERD EN GEDRUKT IN BEZET NEDERLAND. ONVERDRAAGLIJKE LECTUUR VOOR MOFFEN EN N.S.B.'ers.

Onder redactie van alias Brugmans

ER IS 'N PRINSESJE GEBOREN.

Temidden van een wereld vol smart en ellende, temidden van dood en verderf, is een nieuwe, ranke loot aan de oude Oranjeboom ontsproten. Om velerlei redenen stemt deze geboorte ons tot dankbaarheid. Radio, pers, de gesprekken van alledag verluiden ononderbroken van de lugubere heerschappij van den Dood. Millioenen jonge menschen sneuvelen, worden vermoord, worden zinloos vermoord. Het machtige gebod: Gij zult niet dooden!, dat iedereen Zondag in duizenden kerken klakkeloos wordt uitgepreveld door stervelingen die zich dienaren van den Hoogsten God wenschen te noemen, is tot een banale mop verlaagd, 'n ironische opmerking, als om de oppermacht van den duivelschen Dood des te onomstootelijker te doen beseffen. Heel de wereld is één onoverzienbaar massagraf geworden waarin menschen die door menschen worden vermoord, vaneengereten hun rustplaats vinden.

Somber beeld van onze beschaving, somber beeld van den schijnbaren Onmacht van het Christendom, somber beeld van den Almacht van het materialisme.

Als 'n lichtpunt in deze alles-omringende duisternis, is nu 'n Prinsesje geboren, en even staan wij allen stil bij dit schoone wonder der Natuur. Waar millioenen moeders hun kinderen geweldadig moeten verliezen, is hier 'n moeder die het onmetelijke geluk deelachtig wordt een kind te mogen ontvangen. Met Prinses Juliana is het geheele Nederlandsche Volk oprecht dankbaar voor dit wondere blijk van Genade. Wij willen dit zien als een symbool van Nieuw Leven, van Zuivering welke het oude, het erkend verkeerde, vervangt.

Het jaar 1943 geeft den schijn een keerpunt in de geschiedenis der menschheid te zullen worden. De menschheid, met uitzondering van enkele internationale kanonnen-, olie- en geld-koningen, snakt naar de Vrede, snakt er naar om haar met bloed besmeurde handen te mogen reinigen; 'n nieuwe samenleving op te bouwen waarin een diep zedelijk besef de dierlijke instincten die ons belagen, zal overwinnen.

Kleine Margriet, je zult ons Vredesprinsesje zijn. Wij verlangen er naar je in ons midden te hebben, wijl jouw komst ons de zekerheid van de Vrede brengt en Leven beteekent voor duizenden, ja wellicht millioenen jonge menschen.

Kom spoedig Margriet, wij wachten je met open armen....

An underground newspaper in the Netherlands proclaims the electrifying news in January, 1943: "A princess is born."
"Little Margriet," it stated, "you will be our princess of peace. We long to have you in our midst... Come soon, Margriet. We are awaiting you with open arms."

Foreword

Amidst the dark days of World War II when Holland was invaded and occupied, a happy event occurred in Ottawa which brought the beleaguered Dutch a ray of hope. The birth of Her Royal Highness Princess Margriet Francisca, named after the marguerite which blossoms so profusely in Holland, was the auspicious harbinger of better days to come for the Dutch people and a further cementing of the already warm ties existing between Canada and the Netherlands. The future would reveal that the princess's arrival was also to herald the beginning of a particularly close relationship between the two countries.

When Canadian troops liberated the Netherlands in 1945, the Dutch gave enthusiastic expression to their gratitude. It is significant, however, that their appreciation was not confined to their hour of euphoria but continues today in Holland where the graves of Canadian soldiers are still carefully tended by school children. Princess Juliana also thanked the Canadian nation for having provided her and her family with a comfortable refuge during the war by offering our nation's capital a floral gift which has become synonymous with her country: the tulips which bring so much colour to Ottawa and which are a focal point of the city's spring festival are a joyful reminder of Dutch gratitude. Moreover, the princess who was born here has not forgotten her early days in Canada but has enthusiastically taken upon herself the task of promoting the warm bond between the Netherlands and Canada. She has travelled to Canada on numerous occasions and has participated in ceremonies held across the country. She has also maintained ties with the Royal Canadian Legion and her son, Floris, became a godchild of the organization, thus strengthening the relationship between the two countries by a new generation.

The remarkable accomplishments of those early Dutch settlers, many of whom arrived in Canada with little more than a desire to build better lives for their families, provide inspiration for Canadians of all backgrounds. Dutch-Canadians, like people of many other cultural groups, have flourished and prospered in Canada, giving new life to the time-honoured and cherished traditions which have been passed down by their ancestors. Moreover, these aspects of our varied culture remind us not only of what we have achieved, but also of the rich legacy that all Canadians must continue to nurture and protect. May the reading of **When Canada Was Home, The Story of Dutch Princess Margriet** highlight once again this magnificent heritage!

Ramon John Hnatyshyn
Governor General of Canada

Introduction

I take great pleasure in introducing a new book by Albert VanderMey entitled **When Canada was Home**. The book contains an exciting collection of special photographs of Her Royal Highness Princess Margriet taken during her stay in Ottawa.

Princess Margriet, third daughter of former Queen Juliana, was born in Ottawa where the Dutch royal family settled temporarily during the Second World War. The special relationship between this Dutch princess and Canada continued to grow stronger over the years, which is the reason why she is often called the "Canadian princess."

Over the years Princess Margriet has returned to Canada many times for both official and private visits. Her husband, Mr. Pieter van Vollenhoven, shares her love for Canada. Both of them take an active interest in the Canadian Arctic in general and the lives and culture of the Inuit in particular.

In the Netherlands, the Ottawa-born princess is active in social and social-medical work and also fulfills many official functions on behalf of her sister, Queen Beatrix.

In the year I have been in Ottawa, I have come to understand that the memory of our princesses growing up in Ottawa still lives vividly in the minds of many Canadians. It is especially to them that I recommend this book.

G.W. Baron de Vos van Steenwijk
Netherlands Ambassador to Canada

The House of Orange

Princess Margriet, the main subject of this book, belongs to the ancient and enduring House of Orange-Nassau whose roots in the Netherlands date back more than four centuries.

The patriarch of this dynasty is William of Orange, a German-born prince who, in 1544, inherited from a cousin the title to the French principality of Orange and large estates in the Netherlands. He became popularly known as William the Silent for his ability to keep his mouth discreetly shut.

But there was nothing taciturn or mysterious about him when it came to standing up against the autocratic Spaniard rule, and for the freedom of conscience he adhered to, especially when the ruthless Duke of Alva was sent north to teach the "heretics" a lesson.

William quickly emerged as the leader of the forces that fought valiantly for the liberation from the hated Spaniards. He was proclaimed the first *stadhouder*, or governor, of the seven provinces which had united to form a common front in the struggle for independence. Alas, he met death at the hands of an assassin in 1584.

The war against Spain would not end until 1648 - eighty years after it began.

After William the Silent, who is now generally referred to as the father of the fatherland, six more members of the House of Orange would serve as stadhouders: Maurice, Frederick Henry, William II, William III, William IV and William V.

The Netherlands did not get its first king until after the defeat of French conqueror Napoleon Bonaparte at Leipzig, Germany, in 1813. The Dutch revolted and recalled the son of William V from exile, proclaiming him as William I, sovereign king of the Netherlands. Two of his successors were named William II and William III. Little wonder that the average Dutchman today needs to refer to a chart to distinguish the two sets of Williams.

Wilhelmina, the grandmother of Margriet, broke the long line of male succession by becoming queen in 1890 at the tender age of ten. Her mother, Queen Emma, served as regent until the age of majority - 18 - was reached.

Wilhelmina, a conservative, no-nonsense woman, ruled her subjects through two world wars and finally, after fifty years on the throne, abdicated in 1948 to her only child, Juliana, who then was thirty-nine.

The mother of Margriet would become a popular monarch who never lost her grip on her nation's affections, despite a number of controversies involving her immediate family. She and her German-born husband, Prince Bernhard, won wide respect and adulation for carrying on their various duties despite all the adversities, in the true tradition of the House of Orange.

Beatrix, the eldest sister of Margriet, also ran into trouble when she decided to marry a German, Claus von Amsberg. Many people who had experienced the unpleasantries of the German occupation during the Second World War didn't appreciate the fact that the future Dutch prince had been a member of the Hitler Youth organization. During the wedding in Amsterdam in March, 1966, gangs of demonstrators roamed the streets, shouting slogans and throwing smoke bombs.

Beatrix became queen in 1980 when her mother abdicated after a thirty-two-year reign. The ceremony took place on April 30, Juliana's seventy-first birthday, a date that would continue to be celebrated as a national holiday.

In the years since, the new queen and her husband, and their three sons, have endeared themselves to the hearts of most Netherlanders, who still regard the colour orange as a symbol of national pride and patriotism.

Under the provisions of the constitutional monarchy, Beatrix is the head of government, but does not actually govern. The executive power is really in the hands of the ministers who form the cabinet. But the queen is required to review carefully a mountain of documents, including legislative measures, before placing her signature on them. It also is her duty, after elections, to appoint the leader of the winning party as prime minister.

There are many other tasks: receiving hundreds of visitors, making regular working visits to all parts of the country and beyond (including tours of social welfare institutions, hospitals and nursing establishments), officially opening public and private projects, unveiling monuments, attending ceremonies that commemorate important events, being guest of honour at performances of plays and films, dropping in at exhibitions and shows, and so on.

A big event on the busy royal calender each year is what the Dutch call *Prinsjesdag*. On the third Tuesday in September, the monarch travels by a "golden coach" to the parliament buildings in The Hague to read the speech of the throne, an outline of the government's intentions for the coming year. It is a great ceremonial occasion attended by other members of the royal family as well.

The eldest son of Beatrix, Prince Willem-Alexander, who was born in 1967, is first in line to inherit the throne. The two other sons, Johan Friso and Constantijn, are next. Princess Irene, Juliana's second child, gave up her rights, and those of her future children, when she decided to marry Prince Charles Hugo, pretender to the Spanish throne. Margriet therefore is fourth in line of succession.

Shortly before becoming queen, Juliana described her future responsibilities as "a task so difficult that none who had dared to think about it for even a moment would desire it, but also so wonderful that I can only say: who am I that I should be given the right to perform it? The opportunities of working for the common good which I am being granted are so great that, after considerable heart-searching, I have made up my mind to follow the vocation for

The queen and her family enjoy a typical Dutch pastime: a bicycle ride.

Queen Beatrix and het consort, Prince Claus, arrive for the opening of the Dutch Parliament in The Hague in a 'golden coach'.

which my parents took such good care to prepare me."

She has passed on this commitment and dedication to her offspring who are equally determined to carry on the proud traditions of the House of Orange. Princess Margriet, in particular, stands out as a true servant and ambassador who relishes her royal role and carries on a full and fascinating life.

The Dutch, it seems, will be singing *Oranje boven* (Orange above all) for a long time to come.

Albert VanderMey

Bent on his conquest of Europe, German dictator Adolf Hitler ordered his forces to attack the Netherlands, his little neighbour to the west, in the pre-dawn hours of May 10, 1940.

The ensuing battle was unequal.

Vastly outnumbered and outgunned, the valiant defenders capitulated after only five days of often vicious warfare.

A dark cloud descended over the land by the North Sea. It would not be lifted until five years later.

Queen Wilhelmina had fled to England at the height of the fighting to avoid falling into the hands of the Nazis.

The other members of the House of Orange -Crown Princess Juliana, her husband Prince Bernhard and their daughters Princess Beatrix, 2 ½, and Princess Irene, nine months - had arrived there earlier.

The little girl at the right in the photo is Renee, daughter of Martine Roell, Juliana's friend, who had accompanied the royal family to the safer abode. Beatrix and Renee turned out to be ideal playmates.

Martine's husband, Willem, who was Bernhard's private secretary, had stayed behind in the Netherlands to look after the royal possessions.

When even England seemed threatened by heavy bombing raids, it was felt that Juliana's small party would have to move again, farther away from the danger, farther away from the homeland, to ensure the continuity of the House of Orange.

And they would go without Bernhard who would stay at the queen's side in England as long as the struggle for the return of freedom continued.

The chosen land of exile was Canada, an ally far away from the fires that engulfed Europe.

Beatrix and Renee are shown playing on the deck of the Sumatra, the Dutch cruiser which ferried the royal party across the perilous ocean.

The Sumatra, *accompanied by the Dutch destroyer,* Jacob van Heemskerck, *managed to avoid the German U-boats, undersea demons that constantly preyed on Allied vessels, big and small.*

The voyage, in fact, was quite uneventful.

The relieved captain would later describe his special passengers, including the little girls, as "good sailors," who had suffered little or no discomfort during the crossing.

The royal party arrived at the harbour in Halifax, Nova Scotia, on June 11.

A local newspaper, The Herald, marked the occasion with a bit of gossip: "Princess Juliana and her husband, Prince Bernhard, are expecting the birth of a third child soon. If the child is a son, he will be heir to the Netherlands throne."

The report would turn out to be premature. Juliana's pregnancy would not be formally announced until after the summer of 1942.

While en route to Ottawa, the royal party stayed for a week at the secluded Seigniory Club on the Ottawa River near Montebello, Quebec.

In a radio address to the Canadian people, Juliana said of her children: "You will see them in your midst. You will see them quite often, because we don't like locking ourselves up - that is not in our nature. I hope that you will be kind towards them. Just give them a smile. Then they will be happy and will ask for nothing more."

In Ottawa, the fugitives were warmly welcomed by Canada's new Governor General, the Earl of Athlone, and his wife, Princess Alice, who was an aunt of Juliana.

Since an early return to the Netherlands was out of the question, with the Nazis being deeply entrenched, the plan was to rent a house in Rockcliffe Park, a prestigious suburb of the capital.

Until a suitable place was found, Juliana, Martine and the others remained as guests at Government House, the official residence of the viceregal couple.

A house was finally selected. It stood on ten acres of land at 120 Lansdowne Road, somewhat secluded, with the back lawn sloping down to McKay Lake, a small body of water.

It was quickly dubbed "Nooit Gedacht" (We never thought this). After she was settled in, Juliana often went on the road, visiting various places, including the Canadian National Exhibition in Toronto, never failing to draw attention to the sorry plight of her countrymen.

Later, Juliana volunteered regular duty in the Superfluity Shop, a secondhand store which had been set up by a group of women who wanted to raise money for the war effort.

She also did a lot of knitting for the military. And she donated her blood to the Red Cross.

Several institutions of higher learning in the United States honoured her with degrees.

Then there was also the important task of looking after her young family.

Trix, for one, adjusted to life in Canada without difficulty. The future queen is shown taking advantage of the fine weather with a refreshing dip in a neighbourhood pool.

In the winter, her mother took her and Irene on a visit to a maple syrup operation in the bush near Ottawa managed by a religious order.

A year went by before Bernhard got an opportunity to fly across the Atlantic for a reunion with his wife and children.

He vowed to come over more frequently, and did, often in conjunction with military matters.

One of his stops was the Dutch army recruiting and training base in Stratford, Ontario, where he was the guest of Col. G. J. Sas, the commanding officer.

Juliana also visited the troops regularly.

In late spring of 1942, Dr. John F. Puddicombe, chief of the obstretical department at Ottawa's Civic Hospital, received a telephone call from Juliana. She wanted to make an appointment.

The doctor was told to keep the strictest secrecy, as the official announcement would not be made until the fourth month of the pregnancy.

Of course, Queen Wilhelmina was informed right away. The news prompted her to speed up plans for visiting her daughter and granddaughters whom she hadn't seen for two years.

There were tears of happiness when she arrived in Canada on June 18.

That's little Irene with the Indian head-dress, after the conclusion of an outdoor play, and with the red, white and blue ark presented by the children of Lee as a token of all the ships laden with food that would sail from America toward a liberated Netherlands.

Wilhelmina sought out Dr. Puddicombe. "In our family," she told him, "it is expected that one follows orders. We are sufficiently disciplined. From now on, you must telephone me if Juliana refuses to do what you prescribe."

She then turned her attention to the next point on her agenda: a trip to Lee, a placid little town in the U.S. state of Massachusetts, where Juliana had leased a summer home.

The entire royal household, with the exception of the prince, would be spending the summer of 1942 there.

The holiday turned out to be just what the doctor had ordered: a period of relaxation away from the worries and cares of the everyday world.

It was impossible for the royal family to escape from all formalities, however. Wilhelmina, in particular, often received official visitors, and even went to see President Franklin Roosevelt and addressed the U.S. Congress.

There were also photo sessions to satisfy the voracious appetite of the press.

With the vacation at an end, it was business as usual.

Bernhard broke the news of the pregnancy in a broadcast over Radio Orange, which employed the facilities of the BBC in London. The Netherlanders were strongly advised not to openly demonstrate their joy, for fear of causing reprisals. The German occupiers held their neighbours in an iron grip - and their disdain for Wilhelmina and her family was certainly no secret.

Needless to say, Bernhard's warning was not heeded by everyone.

Parts of villages and towns were in ruins, the result of the warfare in 1940, but the spirit of the people remained largely unbroken.

In Ottawa, where winter had settled in, the little exiles frequently romped in the frigid outdoors.
They were too young to fully comprehend what had happened to their homeland - and their family. They had other things on their mind, including the fact that they would soon have a baby brother or sister.

No. 232   **EXTRA**   Vol. LXXVI

THE CANADA GAZETTE
LA GAZETTE DU CANADA

OTTAWA, SATURDAY, DECEMBER 26, 1942 | OTTAWA, SAMEDI 26 DÉCEMBRE 1942

PROCLAMATION

ATHLONE
[L.S.]

CANADA

GEORGE THE SIXTH, by the Grace of God, of Great Britain, Ireland and the British Dominions beyond the Seas KING, Defender of the Faith, Emperor of India.

To ALL TO WHOM these Presents shall come or whom the same may in anywise concern, GREETING:

A PROCLAMATION

F. P. VARCOE, Deputy Minister of Justice, Canada.

WHEREAS it is necessary and advisable, for the security, defence, peace, order and welfare of Canada, that arrangements should be made to enable heads of the United Nations and Royal Families thereof, to take refuge within the territorial limits of Canada, and thus to promote and encourage the war efforts of t' United Nations.

AND WHEREAS, in particular, it is arrangements should be made to e'

PROCLAMATION

ATHLONE
[L.S.]

CANADA

GEORGE SIX par la Grâce de Dieu, Roi de Grande-Bretagne, d'Irlande et des Territoires britanniques au delà des mers, Défenseur de la Foi, Empereur des Indes.

A TOUS CEUX À QUI les présentes parviendront ou qu'icelles pourront de quelque manière concerner,—SALUT:

PROCLAMATION

F.-P. VARCOE, Sous-ministre de la Justice, Canada.

ATTENDU qu'il est nécessaire et utile, pour la sécurité, la défense, la paix, l'ordre et le bien-être du Canada, que des dispositions soient prises pour permettre aux souverains et aux familles royales des Nations unies de se réfugier dans les limites territoriales d' Canada, dans le b' de favoriser l'effort de gu' des Nations unie

ET ATTENDU   en particulier dre des dis'   à la F?

A terrible thought bothered the inner circle: a baby born to Juliana in Canada would have to be registered as a Canadian citizen. If the child were a boy, it would be undesirable to have a future king with Canadian nationality.

To everyone's relief, a legal adviser with the external affairs department came up with a solution. He prepared a document which declared the place of birth as extraterritorial, thus ensuring Dutch citizenship for the newborn.

The proclamation was published in an extra edition of the official Canada Gazette *on December 26, 1942.*

Many people believed that the birth would take place on Dutch soil. There even were reports that real Dutch earth had been brought to Canada and sprinkled about the delivery room at the Civic Hospital.

None of this was true, of course.

The hospital made sure that everything was in order for receiving its distinguished patient.

Four rooms were to be set aside on the third floor: one for Juliana, one for the baby, one for the special nurse and one for the ever-present security agents.

"At first we thought the baby should be with the other babies," Juliana would explain later. "I wanted us to be treated like any other mother and child. But later that didn't seem wise. So many people had to visit her officially, and they might have carried infection to the other babies. It wouldn't have been fair to them."

A charming bassinet, fitted out by some nurses who knew "a little about sewing," stood waiting. It was the usual white-painted, wicker-type cradle on wheels made up in pink silk with point d'esprit done entirely by hand.

In April of 1952, when Juliana, then queen, would make a nostalgic visit to the hospital, the bassinet was spotted immediately. She must have looked at it for most of a minute before moving on.

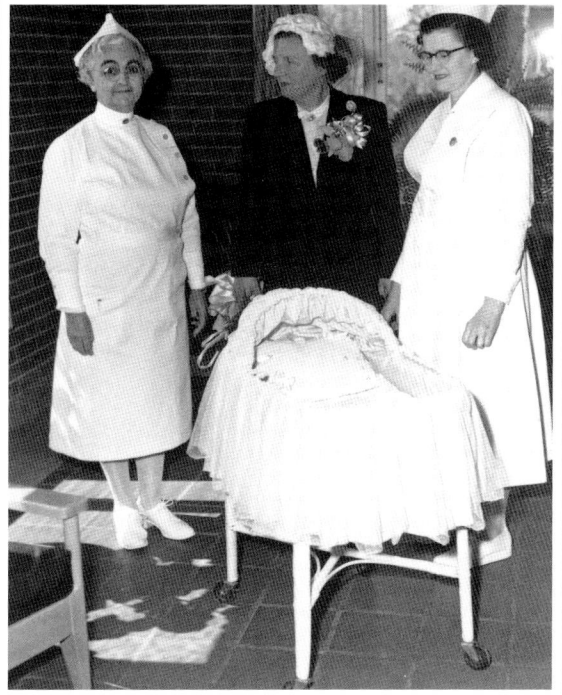

12th January, 1943.

Confidential

To: The Under Secretary of State for External Affairs

From: The Secretary to the Governor General.

      I have shown to The Governor General Mr. Vincent Massey's telegram No. 66 of January 8th. His Excellency's view is that there should be no exception to the Wartime ban on gun salutes. He considers that the birth of a child to Princess Juliana might be recognized by the playing of the Dutch National Anthem on the Carillon in the Peace Tower and perhaps by the display of the Dutch flag on some of the public buildings.

    Bernhard wanted the birth to be celebrated with a bang - one whose reverberations would reach the subjugated people of Holland and instill in them renewed hope that all was not lost and that a brighter future lay ahead.

    Vincent Massey, Canada's top diplomat in London, conveyed the prince's idea to the external affairs department: "Prince Bernhard asked me very privately and informally, and also very diffidently, just before he left London to fly to Canada, if it would be possible to arrange for a salute of guns on the occasion of the birth of the child to their Royal Highnesses. He feels that if this salute could be recorded and broadcast to the people of the Netherlands, together with a message that this child was born on Dutch soil in Canada, such a message would have a great appeal to the hearts of the Dutch people."

    The idea was fine. But it went contrary to Canada's wartime ban on gun salutes. Even the governor general, who was almost a member of the family, believed that no exception should be made.

Juliana, friend Martine and the others in the household had moved bag and baggage to Stornaway, a spacious residence at 541 Acacia Avenue, in the same Rockcliffe Park neighbourhood. It was let fully furnished, down to the linen and silverware.

A larger house was surely needed, especially with a baby on the way.

On the morning of January 18, Dr. Puddicombe picked up his ringing telephone and heard the voice of Juliana.

"How's your sense of humour today?" the princess asked.

"I hope it's all right, Your Royal Highness," the doctor replied. "But what's the matter?"

Juliana then announced matter-of-factly: "I have the mumps."

Trix had been spreading them around.

The doctor didn't waste any time in ordering his patient to the hospital. She was expected to go into labour any time and he certainly did not want any complications.

    Shortly after 7 p.m. on Tuesday, January 19, the telephone rang in the reception room of the stately Chateau Laurier hotel in downtown Ottawa where reporters were anxiously awaiting word of the birth.

    A Dutch information officer from Montreal picked up the receiver and quickly announced: "Gentlemen, the baby is born. It's a girl."

    There was a collective gasp. Then everyone ran for the phones to spread the news around the world. Some of the reporters would dub the baby, somewhat romantically and wistfully, Canada's princess.

    Bernhard, who was at the hospital, immediately informed Wilhelmina by telephone.

    "I'm so happy," the queen said, when told that everything had gone well. "I am very, very happy. Give Juliana a kiss for me."

    The hospital issued its first communique at 7:45: "The princess is doing extremely well. The little princess is a healthy baby of seven pounds, twelve ounces, which is five ounces more than average weight."

    The next day, carillonneur Robert Donnell made the bells in the Peace Tower of the Parliament Buildings ring out joyously in the frosty air with the sound of Dutch songs, including the national anthem.

    And high above the tower, the red, white and blue of the Dutch flag fluttered in the wind.

    It was the first time a foreign flag had flown alone from the seat of Canada's government.

One of Juliana's near neighbours when she lived on Lansdowne Road, Hoyes Lloyd of 582 Mariposa Avenue, hauled out his huge Dutch flag, which he had acquired on his travels, and displayed it prominently on his front lawn.

After two girls, Juliana had been hoping that the next child would be a boy. That was an open secret.

But if there was any disappointment over the birth of yet another girl, this wasn't noticeable.

The father would explain later over Radio Orange: "Just like any other family, we would have found it nice to have a son after two daughters. But you could have imagined our happiness if you had seen our sweet little girl. Even before my wife had seen her, she said to me: 'I'm really glad it's a girl. If it had been a son, perhaps there would have been too much excitement in Holland and even victims. Now I can breathe easier.'"

At 3:27 p.m., somewhat behind schedule - it was baby's feeding time - Bernhard carried his new daughter into the sunroom, a few steps from where Juliana was recuperating, for the official registration.

The baby, soundly asleep, wore a white organdie dress and was lying on a pillow covered with old lace.

The proceedings were brief and simple. One Canadian reporter described them as follows: "A mere recording of the birth of a child carried out by the prince exactly as it is done by every Dutch commoner who leaves his clacking windmill and trudges though his poppy-blown field to the nearest burgomaster's house in Holland."

G. P. Luden of Montreal, the Dutch consul general, read the official Act.

The prince and two official witnesses - F. E. H. Groenman, the Dutch minister to Canada, and Willem van Tets, Juliana's private secretary - then signed the register, using a white and gold fountain pen belonging to Dr. Puddicombe.

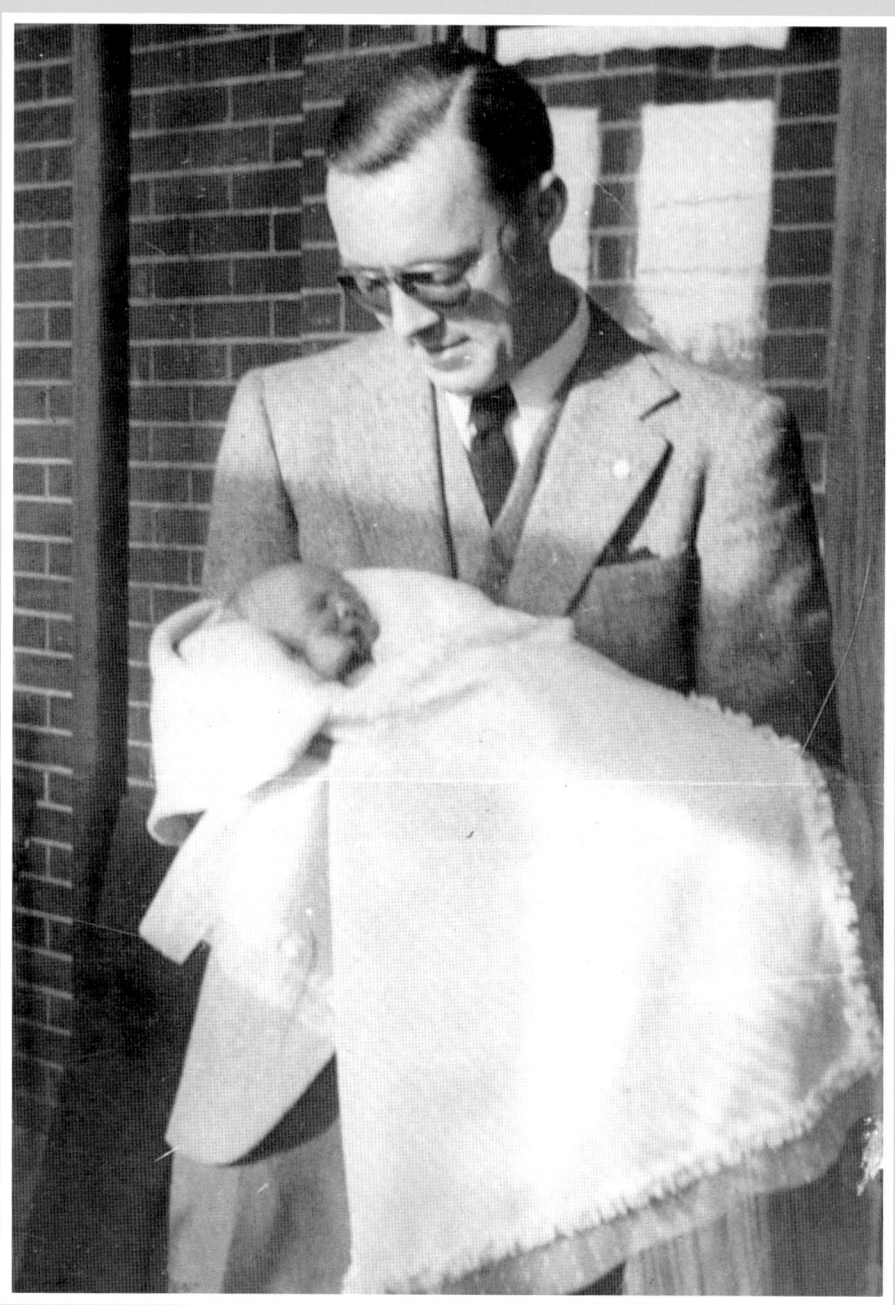
The baby's name: Margriet Francisca.

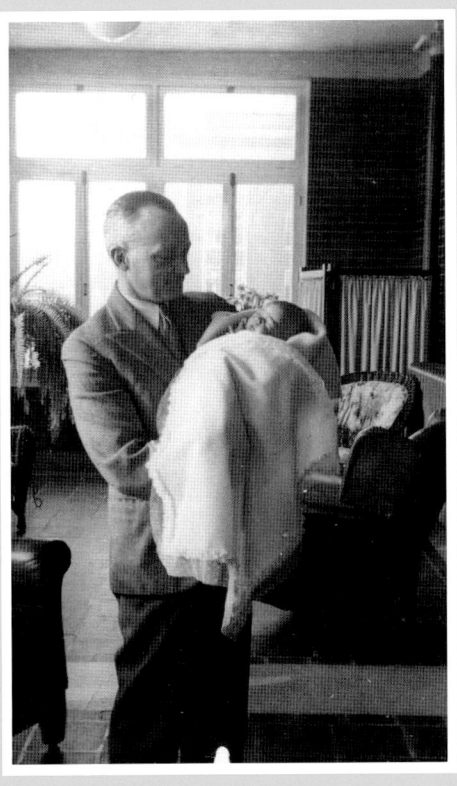

The traditional serving of rusks spread with orange aniseed (beschuit met muisjes) *was handed out liberally, thanks to a special order to the firm of Edward Jurgens in Brooklyn, New York.*

Dr. Puddicombe got some, too, neatly wrapped in orange paper with a red, white and blue ribbon.

One reporter took a bite and described his rusk "as hard as a chunk of the city's ice-encrusted pavement." Another remarked: "With rationing what it is, these taste pretty good."

Little Margriet was named after the marguerite flower which her grandmother had selected as a symbol of resistance and hope.

In one of her memorable broadcasts over Radio Orange, Wilhelmina explained: "It is the intention of the parents through their choice of a name to establish a lifelong bond between our grievously tried people in the occupied part of the kingdom and the newly-born. Before our mind rises the image of the treacherous assault of the Huns on our country and of the struggle against the Japanese for our beautiful East Indies. Who does not remember the marguerites budding in the month of May in the meadows and fields, reclothing with their whiteness every year the memory of the suffering and grief of those terrible days in 1940 and whispering of a better future? But above all, the name is a reverent tribute to the memory of our heroes on land and sea, no matter in what part of the world they may have fallen, and to those who died as martyrs for their country's cause. May their memory live not only in our hearts but also through the new great happiness which God has given my children...."

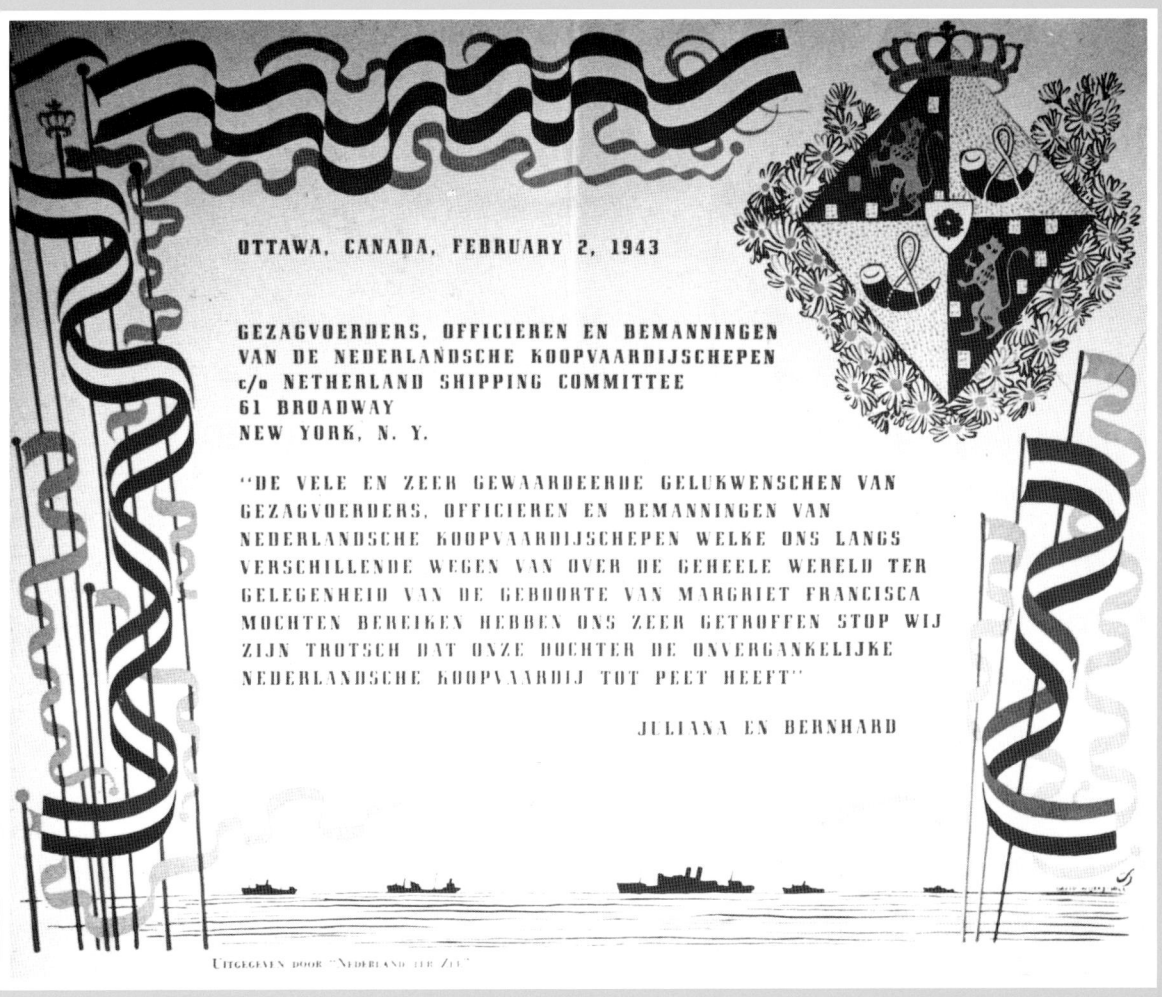

Congratulatory messages and gifts poured into Ottawa from all corners of the world.

Juliana and Bernhard were particulary fond of the well wishes received from the Dutch merchant marine. After Holland's capitulation in May, 1940, the ships and crews in foreign ports and on the high seas had continued to sail under British command, lending invaluable assistance to the allied effort.

The royal couple drafted a special thank you.

Trix and Irene eagerly looked forward to seeing the new member of their family. They finally got the opportunity when Dad took them to the hospital for a brief visit.

Three months later, listeners of Radio Orange would hear sweet voices: "It is the dearest baby in the whole world"; "She's already playing with her hands"; "I've made a necklace for her, one this big."

The children were required to keep up their Dutch at home - unless English-speaking guests were present - and various Dutch customs.

After all, they were in Canada only temporarily, and would head home as soon as peace had been restored.

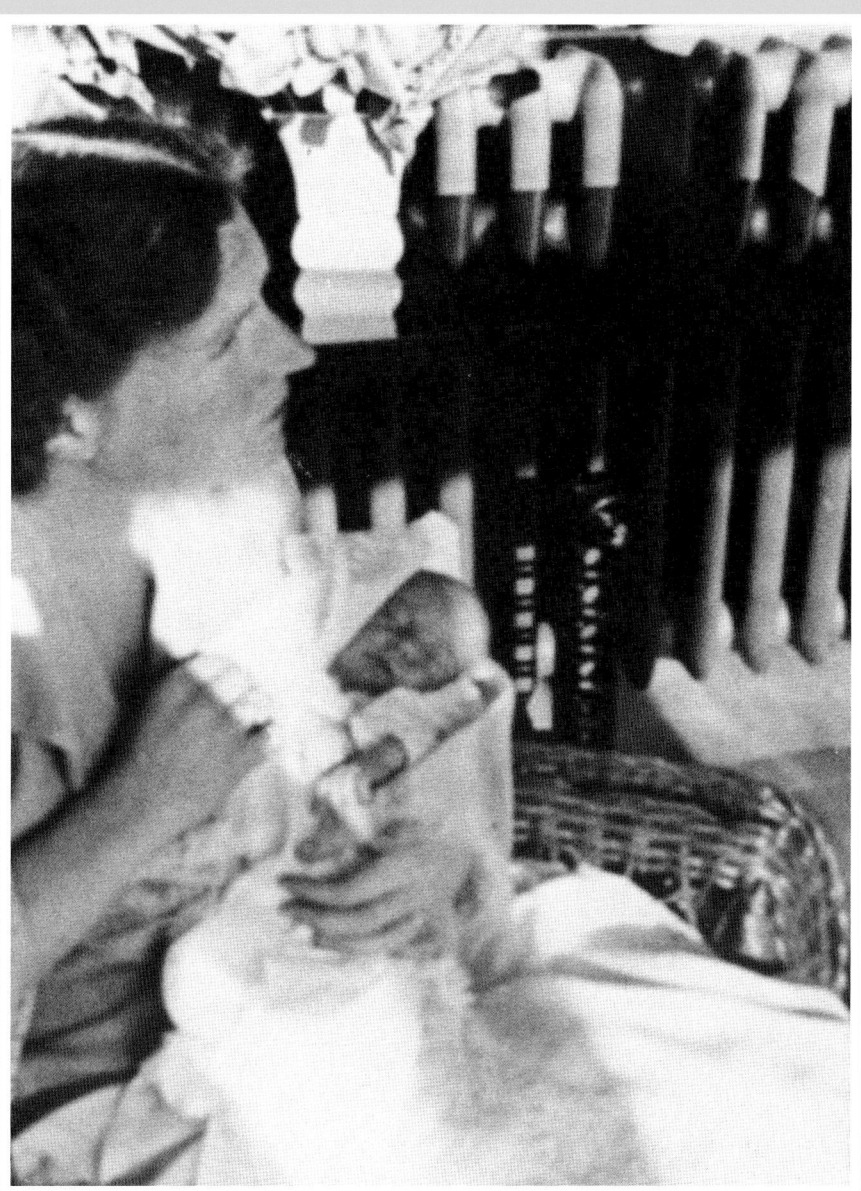

U.S. President Roosevelt was proud of his Dutch ancestry. He once wrote: "Our early forbears brought from the Netherlands a quality of endurance against great odds - a quality of quiet determination to conquer obstacles of nature and man."

He felt a close relationship with the royal family, particularly Wilhelmina. Little wonder that he was honoured by being named one of Margriet's godparents.

The others were Queen Mary of England, the Earl of Athlone, Martine Roell, who could be identified only as the widow of a Netherlander "who died as a martyr for his country," so as not to provoke reprisals against her relatives in Holland, and all the personnel of the revered merchant marine. Martine's husband had been executed by the Germans.

The advice not to demonstrate openly certainly didn't apply to people outside the Netherlands.

For many, the royal birth was the happiest news to come along in years. It gave them an opportunity to vent their pent-up emotions and focus on something other than rations and the latest reports from the war zones.

"For us, 1943 is the year of our rising hope," declared F. E. H. Groenman, the Dutch minister to Canada, at a reception at his home in Ottawa.

In London, Pieter S. Gerbrandy, prime minister of the exiled Dutch government, said: "This new proof that the royal house flourishes awakens the greatest joy and gratitude in Netherlanders."

A commemorative plate showing the various parts of the kingdom quickly became a best seller.

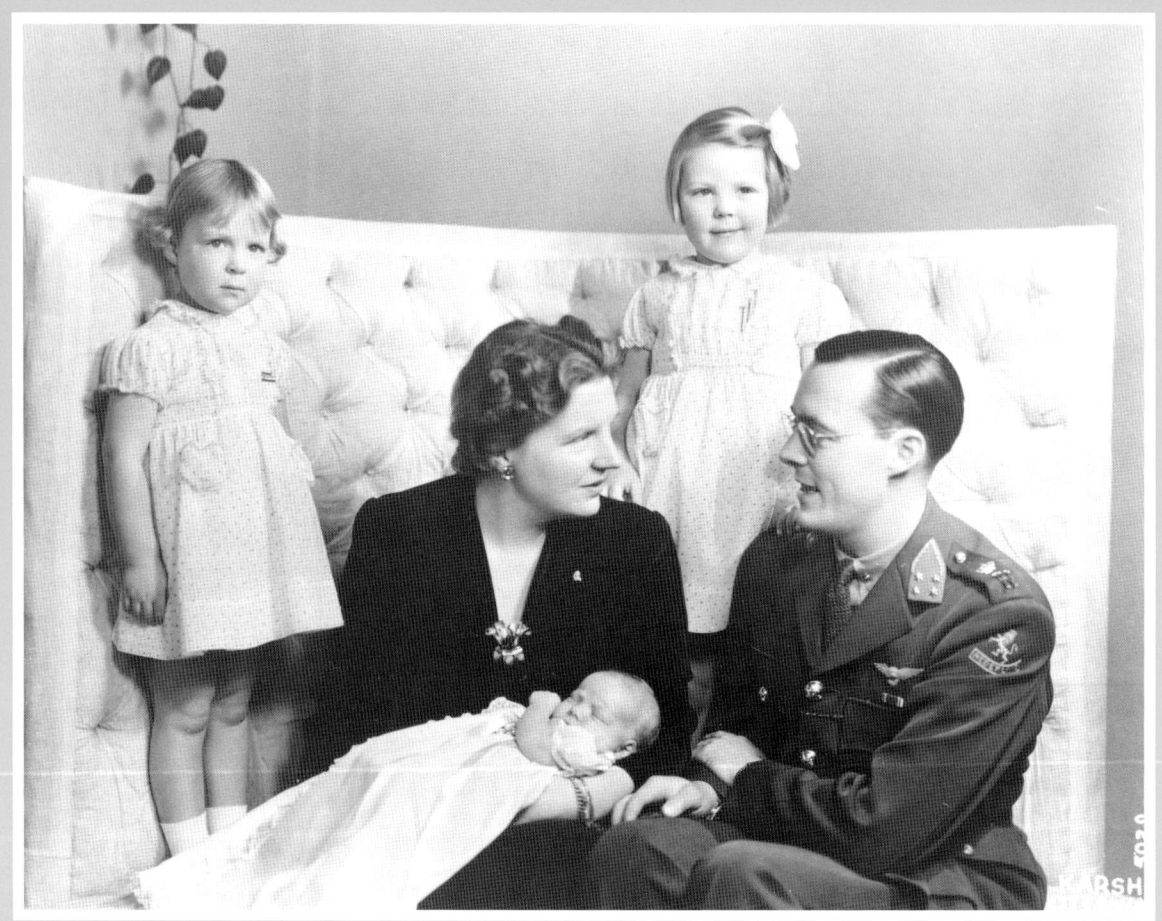

Juliana must have been very pleased with Dr. Puddicombe's comments to a reporter shortly after he had paid a goodnight visit to Margriet.

"Oh my, she's beautiful," he had said. "I'm not just saying that because she's Princess Juliana's child. She'd be perfect no matter who her parents were. She's got quite a bit of silky hair already. And I think it's going to be curly from the way it looks now. Her eyes are blue, like her mother's and little sisters'. Her bones are good and her body is beautifully proportioned. And, oh my, is she a chubby little thing."

"I found the royal couple and their children a close and homeloving family," recalled Gladys Moorhead, a nurse at the Civic Hospital who had accompanied Juliana back to her home to help with the care of the baby. "They spoke Dutch when they were with one another, but if I or some other English-speaking person was nearby, all of them, even the young children, would switch to English. They always were very polite. The only time when I fully realized that I was living in a special household was when I would go out and, upon my return, had to satisfy two guards at the door that I did have a right to enter."

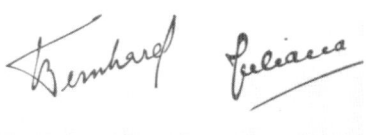

The thank you cards and personal messages sent out by the royal couple would become cherished possessions.

Margaret Humphry, night nurse at the hospital, received a letter from Juliana which stated: "I feel so happy whenever I go over my hospital memories, which I so often do, and I do want to thank you again for your part in it. Every time I think of the first night there, I must laugh, and I get downright sentimental whenever I think of the chocolate milk and how lovely that was in the night... Margriet is flourishing. More of a child and less of a baby. More obviously a personality. Everything is going according to wish...."

The other children were flourishing, too.

*Baptismal Service
of
Her Royal Highness Princess Margriet Francisca
of the Netherlands
at St. Andrew's Church
Ottawa
Tuesday, June 29th 1943
at 1:00 P.M.*

*This card is not transferable.   Please present this card at the door.
Doors open at 12:30 P.M.*

Wilhelmina made her second trip to Canada in June, 1943.

She spent most of the time at Juliana's house, admiring the baby and taking a well-deserved rest.

A highlight of her visit would be Margriet's christening on June 29, Bernhard's 32nd birthday.

The ceremony in St. Andrew's, the downtown Presbyterian church where Juliana regularly attended services, would be witnessed by more dignitaries than any other event in Ottawa since the start of the war.

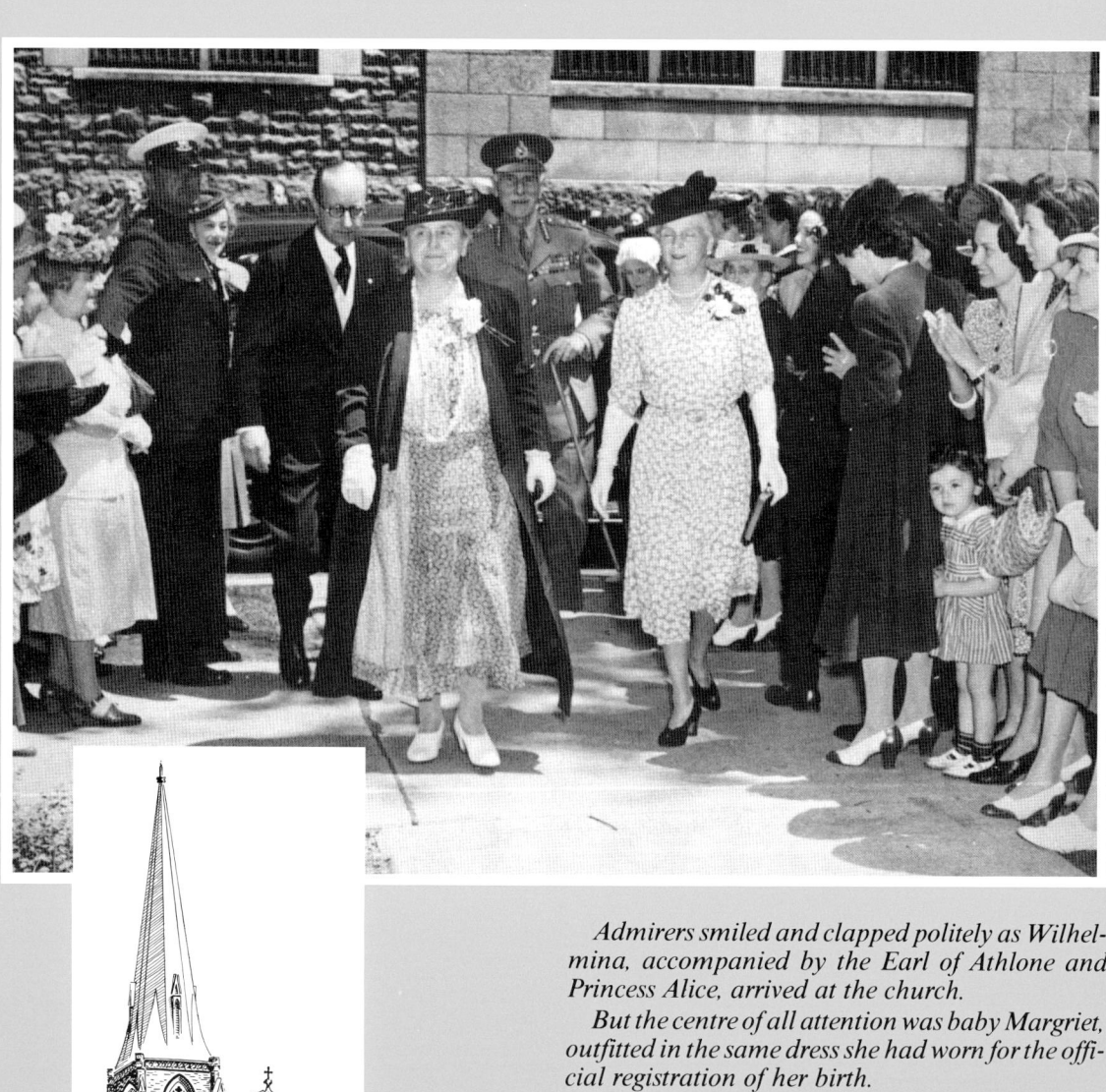

Admirers smiled and clapped politely as Wilhelmina, accompanied by the Earl of Athlone and Princess Alice, arrived at the church.

But the centre of all attention was baby Margriet, outfitted in the same dress she had worn for the official registration of her birth.

Orde van den Dienst

tot Bediening van den Heiligen Doop

aan

Margriet Francisca

Prinses der Nederlanden

in de St. Andrew's Presbyterian Church

Ottawa

29 Juni 1943

Order of Service

for the Administration of the Sacrament of Baptism

to

Margriet Francisca

Princess of the Netherlands

in St. Andrew's Presbyterian Church

Ottawa

June 29, 1943

Minister
Rev. Dr. Winfield Burggraaff

VOTUM

GEZANG *De Gemeente staat*

Wilt heden nu treden voor God den Heere,
Hem boven al loven van herten seer,
End' maken groot sijns lieven naemens eere,
Die daer nu onsen vijant slaet terneer.

Ter eeren ons Heeren wilt al U dagen
Dit wonder bijsonder gedencken toch;
Maeckt u, o mensch! voor God steets wel te dragen,
Doet yder recht en wacht u voor bedrog.

Bid, waket end' maket dat g'in bekoring
End' 't quade met schade toch niet en valt,
U vroomheijt brengt de vijant tot verstoring,
Al waer sijn rijck noch eens soo sterck bewalt.

SCHRIFTLEZING

GEBED

GEZANG *De Gemeente staat*

Lof zij den Heer den Almachtigen Koning der eere
Dat aard en hemel den lof Zijner glorie vermeere
Meng in 't geklank
Ziel, Uw aanbiddenden dank
Roem al wat ademt den Heere.

Loof nu den Heer, Die niet ophoudt u daaglijks te zeeg'nen
Stroomen der liefde laat Hij uit den Hemel u reeg'nen,
Die in veel nood
En in gevaren zoo groot
U nu met gunst komt bejeeg'nen.

TOESPRAAK

FORMULIER VOOR DE BEDIENING VAN HET SACRAMENT
VAN DEN HEILIGEN DOOP

BEDIENING VAN HET SACRAMENT *De Gemeente staat*

GEZANG

Mijn schilt ende betrouwen
Sijt ghy, o Godt, mijn Heer!
Op U soo wil ick bouwen,
Verlaet mij nimmermeer!
Dat ick doch vroom mach blijven,
U dienaar t'aller stondt,
Die tyranny verdrijven,
Die my myn hert doorwont.

ZEGEN

The service, mostly in Dutch, was led by Rev. Dr. Winfield Burggraaff, a Dutch navy chaplain and minister of the Reformed Church on Staten Island, New York.

Dr. Burggraaff told the parents: "When, in a little while, you approach the baptismal font, you will there be surrounded by the godparents who promise to stand by you, some of them representatives of the great world powers, others of them representing the thousands of men in our merchant navy who do their duty to queen and country in the midst of great danger, all these long and dreadful years. Truly, you are surrounded with love, and in the hearts of our people you have a large place."

Seven men had been picked to represent the merchant marine.

There was some hope that Margriet would utter a few sounds for those in Holland who could listen to a rebroadcast of the service over Radio Orange.

No luck. Margriet would emit only one small gurgle of delight, too faint to be picked up by the microphone.

The wide-eyed youngsters stood on tiptoe to see Dr. Burggraaff sprinkle tiny drops of water on Margriet's forehead.

Each of the royal children now had been baptized in a different country: Beatrix in the Netherlands, Irene in England, just prior to the transatlantic voyage, and Margriet in Canada.

Hundreds of people cheered and applauded enthusiastically when the royal family moved outside after the conclusion of the service.

One day, some Dutch sailors came to Stornaway to pay their respects to the visiting queen.
Margriet was in her playpen, gurgling and sighing, trying very hard to turn over.
"I wonder when she will succeed," the queen remarked.

One of her guests offered: "It won't take her long."
"How do you know?" the queen asked.
"She's one of the House of Orange," he replied, "and they don't give up before they have reached their goal."
Wilhelmina smiled and said softly: "Thank you very much."

Wij Wilhelmina, *bij de gratie Gods,*

Koningin der Nederlanden, Prinses van Oranje-Nassau, enz., enz., enz.

Op de voordracht van Onzen Minister van Buitenlandsche Zaken, Kabinet van den Minister, No. Dec. 4e/17828, van 24 Juli 1943;

HEBBEN GOEDGEVONDEN EN VERSTAAN:

Te benoemen in de Orde van Oranje Nassau tot Officier

Dr. JOHN F. PUDDICOMBE.

Onze Minister van Buitenlandsche Zaken is belast met de uitvoering van dit Besluit, waarvan afschrift zal worden gezonden aan den Kanselier der Nederlandsche Orden.

Londen, 29 Juli 1943.

w.g. WILHELMINA.

De Minister van Buitenlandsche Zaken,
w.g. E.N. van Kleffens.

Voor eensluidend afschrift,
De Minister van Algemeene Zaken a.i.,
Voor dezen,
De Th. Raad-Adviseur,

After the birth, Wilhelmina had sent a cable to Dr. Puddicombe, saying she was glad "everything went so well and I am grateful for your good work."

She was so grateful, in fact, that she made the doctor an Officer of the Order of Orange-Nassau in recognition of his unusual services to the royal family.

At a ceremony at the Dutch legation in Ottawa in early September, he was told: "The fate of the Dutch nation depended on your abilities."

Juliana later would describe the stay in Canada as "wonderful for the children - the air so clean, the lawns so green, and the sunshine so warm."

"Canadians are so nice," Juliana told a visitor while taking a break from her motherly chores. "After the baby was born, we were flooded with telegrams and flowers. I was so touched by the big gifts from Canadian societies to Netherlands relief. It was so nice, and so many of them had no special link with Holland. They didn't know me particularly, but they were so kind. Canada has shown me the greatest hospitality I have ever known."

A baby in the house, and all the extra work and attention that was required, didn't prevent Juliana from continuing her duties on behalf of her country, whether it was greeting airmen who had flown in from the Dutch training base in Jackson, Mississippi, or making a goodwill visit to Curacao, a Dutch island in the Caribbean.

In late October, Margriet had her picture taken for the royal Christmas greeting card.

One Ottawa newspaper reported: "Margriet Francisca graciously posed for the photographer under the subdued floodlight, with the ease and composure of any Hollywood star.

"She quickly took up positions ranging from cooing on her tummy to standing on chubby legs, reaching for her favourite velvet bunny. The happy princess had smiles for everyone in the room and, unlike the average baby, she didn't utter a whimper when she arrived 'on location' to be confronted by strange people and still stranger-looking lights and those contraptions called cameras. As a matter of fact, she practically ignored the photographer as she was busy passing out captivating smiles to her mother, her favourite nurse, Miss Feith, and Mr. van Tets, private secretary to Princess Juliana."

Sophia Feith, the children's nanny, who had stayed at Juliana's side during the exile, wrote to Wilhelmina: "The girls are making big plans about what they're going to do later in Holland. Trix's ideal is to become a farmer and bring pails of milk around to all the children who have had to do without it for all these years."

The news from the war fronts was good. The Germans were being routed in many places.

On June 6, 1944, the Allies stormed the beaches of Normandy, France, and launched an all-out drive to bring about total defeat for Adolf Hitler and his hordes.

Maybe, just maybe, the little princesses would soon be able to step onto liberated Dutch soil.

Realizing that hectic times lay ahead, Juliana took her family to a summer home on the Atlantic coast, at Chatham, Massachusetts, for a well-deserved rest.

Margriet and the others wasted no time in sampling the beach and enjoying the fresh air blowing in off the ocean.

The vacation at Cape Cod provided an ideal opportunity for some family photographs.

The formal clothes looked out of place in the beach setting. They probably were quickly replaced with more casual wear after the photographer's departure.

"My baby will always be a link with Canada," Juliana told an interviewer, "not only for my own family but for the Netherlands."

Most of the formal photos of the royal family in Ottawa were taken by Armenian-born Yousuf Karsh, widely regarded as one of the best portrait photographers in the world.

Many of his pictures were duplicated in the thousands and dropped over the Netherlands by Allied aircraft.

The flow of good news came to an abrupt end when the advancing Allies were stopped at the big rivers in the Netherlands. An early victory was now out of the question.

Most of the country would have to endure another winter of occupation - an extremely terrible one, with people starving to death.

And the princesses would have to spend more of their childhood in exile.

There were diversions from the gloominess: Sinterklaas, the Dutch Santa, stopped by as usual (he is shown during an earlier visit) and there were the merry birthday parties, with their sleigh rides, to which many of the neighbourhood playmates were invited.

In the spring of 1945, the grownups were smiling again. The collapse of Germany, and the liberation of the Netherlands, appeared imminent.

Juliana, who had gone to England in the fall to be at her mother's side in the event of an Allied breakthrough, only to be disappointed, made preparations to go overseas once again.

The children, meanwhile, went about their daily lives as if nothing out of the ordinary was afoot. Trix and Renee continued to attend regular class at the public school.

Margriet probably was a bit confused over all the excitement.

The Germans capitulated in early May, 1945. People in Ottawa went wild with joy and relief and organized a victory parade.

In the Netherlands, the liberated citizens poured out their gratitude for the Allied soldiers, many of whom hailed from Canada.

It was roundup time, too. German soldiers, members of the fascist NSB party and other unreliable elements were flushed out and taken into custody by members of the underground who had been organized into an auxiliary force known as the BS.

These photos show a German nicknamed Scheermes (Razor) and a suspected Dutch collaborator at the spot in the Wieringermeer polder where an active member of the resistance had been shot in the back and buried in a shallow grave.

In September, 1944, the government-in-exile in London had established the BS by amalgamating the three main resistance groups and placing Margriet's father in over-all command.

Juliana had a parting gift for St. Andrew's, the place of Margriet's baptism: a lectern of unpolished oak, bearing the royal coat-of-arms and carvings of marguerites and the four evangelists.

At the dedication service, Rev. Andrew Ian Burnett, the minister, said: "Let this lectern then stand in this place as the abiding memorial of God's gift to a great House and nation in its hour of need."

Juliana also would donate thousands of tulip bulbs to Ottawa in appreciation of the city's kind hospitality.

The photo shows (from the left) Renee, her mother Martine Roell, Margriet, Juliana, nanny Sophia Feith, Beatrix and Irene.

Juliana had left her children in Canada while she made an emotional visit to her homeland.

Now she was back to take them, and the others in the household, to their real home.

"It makes me sad to leave," Juliana told a group of journalists. "Five years is a long time, and one becomes attached. We have made so many friends. We shall leave such happy memories."

The return trip included a stop in Montreal.

In New York, the princesses bade farewell from the RCA building and then boarded a transatlantic liner for the crossing to England.

On August 4, 1945, at a little airfield at Teuge in the Netherlands, Bernhard welcomed his family home.

All eyes were on Margriet. She was a novelty of sorts: a Dutch princess born in a foreign land, setting foot on Dutch soil for the first time.

The spacious Soestdijk Palace near Baarn, which was built in the seventeenth century, was Margriet's new home.

There she enjoyed the carefree innocence of childhood while, in subtle ways, preparing herself for her future role in the House of Orange.

Sometimes she and her sisters had to fend for themselves - under supervision, of course - when Mom and Dad were away to perform their various duties. One such occasion was the nostalgic tour of Canada and the U.S. in 1952.

Juliana found there were a lot more Netherlanders in Canada than when she had said goodbye in 1945.

Tens of thousands had immigrated since the doors to Canada were opened in 1947.

Of course, most of them retained a soft spot for their land of birth, including the culture, the cuisine -and the House of Orange.

Margriet, by the way, stopped being the youngest member of the royal family on February 18, 1947, with the arrival of a new sister, Maria Christina.

The little princess is the centre of attention in this family photo taken in the early 1950s.

At first, she was called Marijke, but later, at her own request, Christina.

In October, 1968, she would go to Montreal to study music, knowing that her mother and sisters had enjoyed so much freedom in Canada during the war.

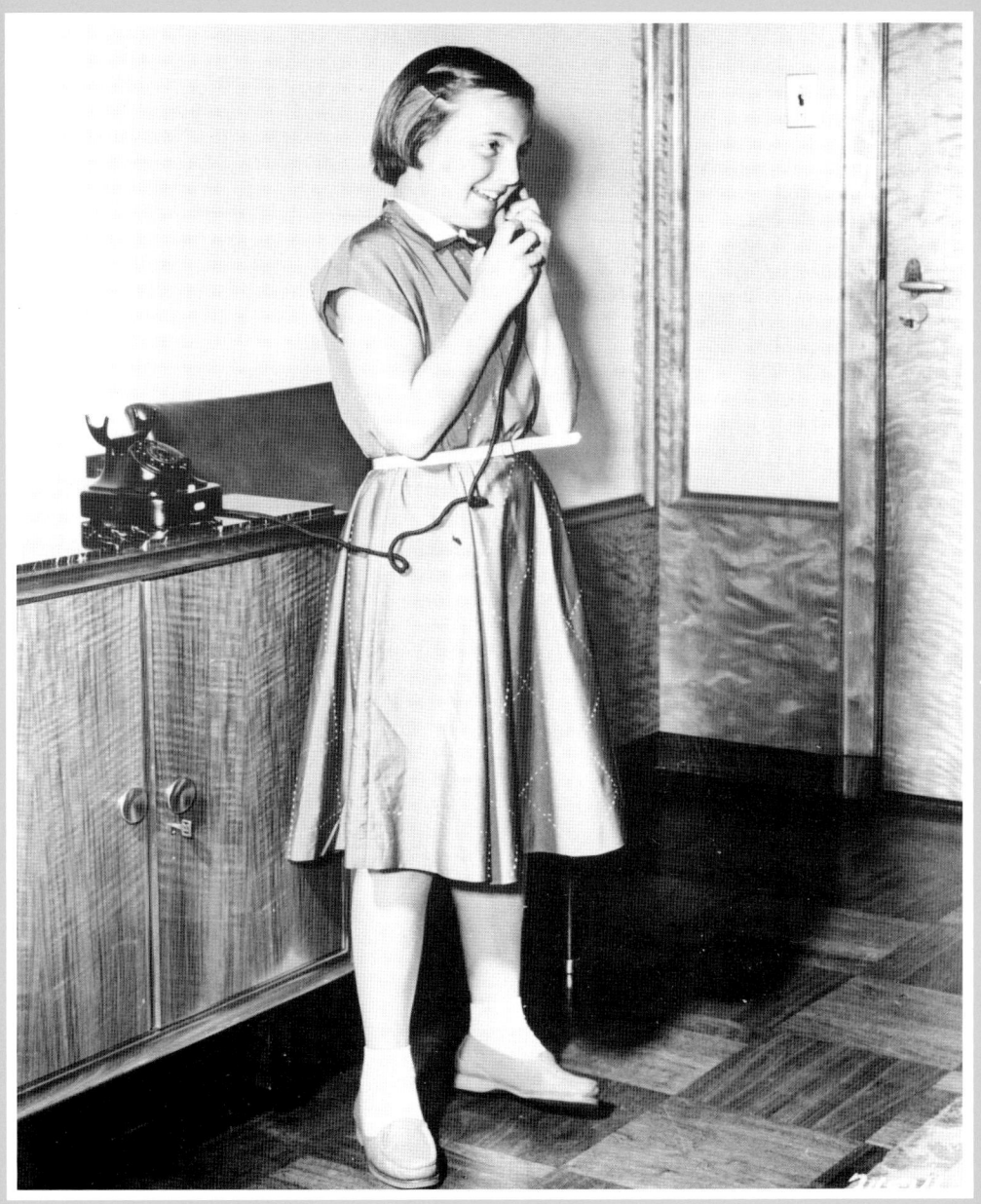

Time flew. Suddenly - well, looking back it seemed suddenly - Margriet was a teenager, whiling away the time on the telephone just like anyone else of her generation.

In March, 1965, Juliana announced Margriet's engagement to Pieter van Vollenhoven, a commoner, one of her daughter's fellow students at the university in Leiden.

It was the first time ever that a princess of the House of Orange had become engaged to someone of Dutch nationality.

The happy couple were married in The Hague on January 10, 1967. Among the many guests were Princess Alice, the Countess of Athlone, and Dr. Burggraaff, who had presided at Margriet's baptism.

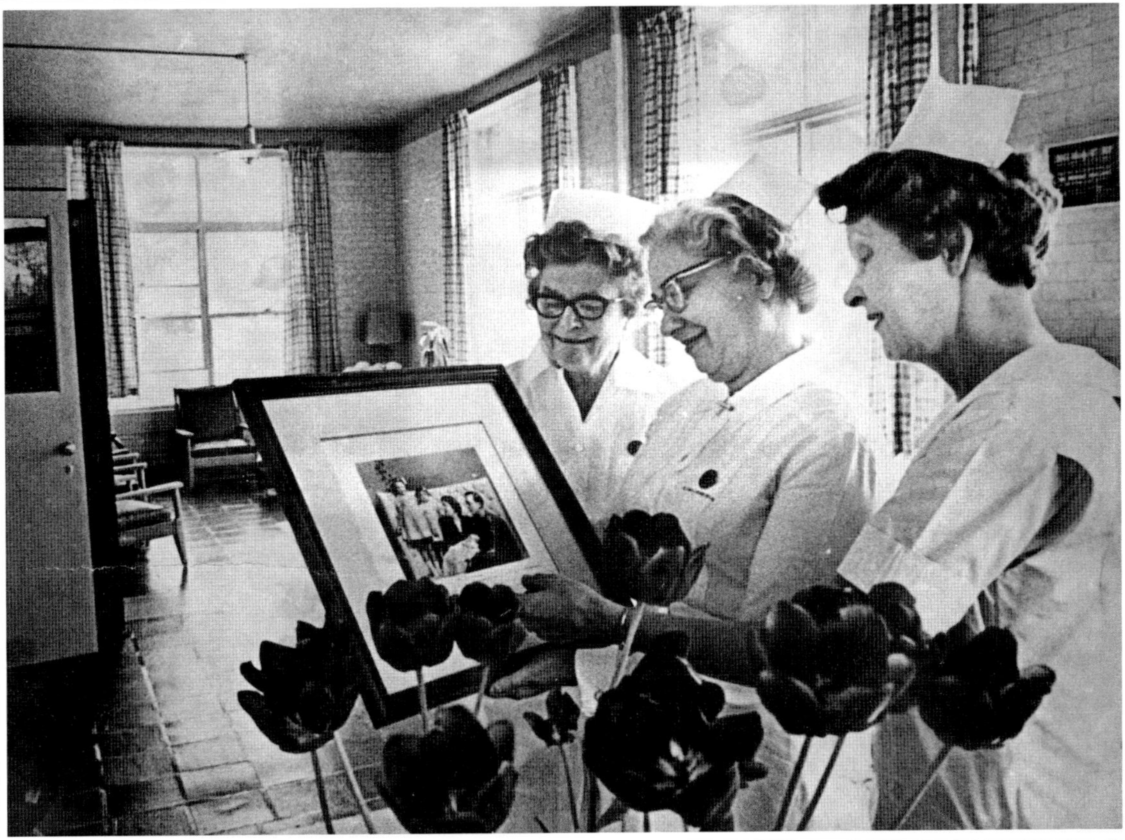

The Dutch flag flew at the Civic Hospital in Ottawa when Margriet gave birth to her first child, Maurits, in April of 1968.

According to her wish, the traditional rusks were passed around freely among staff and patients.

Meanwhile, some of the nurses reflected on another birth that had taken place 25 years earlier.

Three more sons would follow: Bernard in 1969, Pieter-Christiaan in 1972 and Floris in 1975.

When Margriet and her husband visited Canada in September, 1968, she was quite curious to know if she'd feel any twinge of recognition upon driving past the Acacia Avenue house she had lived in for more than two years.

"I wonder... maybe if I see it, it'll come back," she mused. "A friend of mine left Ottawa when she was two, and when she saw a picture of the Gatineau hills, she recalled the view."

But the house rung no more bells in Margriet's mind than did any of the other villas that came into view.

During her visit to the hospital, however, she did recognize something: the sunroom in the maternity suite.

"I've looked at it many times in the family album back home."

The princess and her husband also went to St. Catharines, in the Niagara Peninsula, to attend a performance of the one-man show of Dutch comedian Toon Hermans.

The theatre gave her higher billing on its outdoor display than the popular star.

She was also No. 1 as far as the little girl with the flowers was concerned.

The show was arranged by the Dutch-Canadian Alliance of Ontario, an umbrella organization for a number of credit unions in the province. Its president was John Bosch (at right), a former schoolmate of Margriet at the experimental 'De Werkplaats' in Bilthoven operated by pedagogue Kees Boeke.

After the show, the royal couple had an opportunity to chat with their famous compatriot. The three-week visit included stops at Calgary, Alberta, and the nearby Rocky Mountains.

Margriet has returned to the land of her birth many times.

Most of her visits were strictly for formal occasions. But she has also travelled privately.

Three times - in 1970, 1978 and 1979 - she and her husband went to the far north, away from the crowds and niceties, to spend time with the Inuit. At Somerset Island, in the Northwest Territories, the couple hunted with the native people and lived with them in igloos. Their experiences and observations were recorded in a book back home.

During one stop in Ottawa, the princess asked to meet with Mrs. Puddicombe, the pediatrician's widow.

"I got some advance notice," the elderly woman recalled, "did some hectic tidying-up and there she was at the door to my apartment, smiling from ear to ear. We had a pleasant chat over tea."

In 1974, Margriet and her husband were in Toronto to celebrate the inauguration of direct KLM flights between Amsterdam and Toronto.

In 1986, Vancouver's centennial year, the couple accompanied a trade mission aboard the first direct KLM flight from Amsterdam to Vancouver.

The princess exuded radiance at a press conference held in the Toronto airport's VIP room.

Her itinerary for the next few days included a visit to the awesome waterfalls at Niagara.

On a whirlwind visit to Ottawa in 1978, she found time to tour the Red Cross building with its blood labs, research labs and donation clinic, all areas in which she had a profound interest. She also stopped in Edmonton and Jasper, in Alberta, before heading north to Yellowknife and Resolute Bay.

She returned for yet another time the following year - this time to present a cheque on behalf of her mother to the Civic Hospital's fund-raising campaign for a multi-million-dollar expansion.

"It's a joyous occasion to be back in this hospital today," she said. "It's a hospital that has a special place in our hearts."

In 1982, Margriet and Pieter stopped in Langley, British Columbia, to officially open a vast greenhouse complex called Western Lettuce Now Inc.

This enterprise, covering three hectares, is owned by a number of shareholders of Dutch origin, including former B.C. premier William Vander Zalm.

It stemmed from a special mission in 1980 of the Netherlands Council for Trade Promotion. Contact was made with Vander Zalm, an immigrant's son and then the province's minister of municipal affairs. His enthusiastic response led to development of the project.

As premier, Vander Zalm became the most widely known person of Dutch descent in Canada.

She and her husband were back in 1983 for a variety of official functions.

After a stay in Quebec and a visit to the Parliament Buildings in Ottawa, they headed for Toronto to attend the opening ceremonies at the Art Gallery of Ontario of the exhibition "Dutch Painting of the Golden Age" from the royal collection at the Mauritshuis gallery in The Hague.

Later in the day, the royal couple went to nearby Brampton to take part in the groundbreaking for the 120-bed Faith Nursing Home at Holland Christian Homes, a complex for senior citizens.

Jack Botma and his daughter Shirley of Wyoming, Ontario, were on hand with an open carriage and a pair of their Frisian horses to lend a ceremonial touch to the occasion.

Margriet became known as a roving ambassador who takes great pleasure, and pride, in reinforcing the close ties between the Netherlands and Canada.

In 1990, Margriet and her husband were in Vancouver as special guests at the annual convention of the Royal Canadian Legion. It was 45 years ago that Canadian soldiers, many of whom are still alive and members of the Legion, helped to kick the remaining Germans out of the Netherlands.

During a brief ceremony at the cenotaph in Victoria Square, a few blocks from the convention centre, the royal couple placed a wreath on behalf of the Dutch people.

Later, the princess remarked: "It is important that the younger people are aware of the significance that the Canadians put on the liberation of our country and of the heroic actions that led to it. At the same time, there was the generosity offered to my mother when we lived in Ottawa, where I was born."

Margriet praised the Legion's work with youth and spoke of son Floris who is a godson of the organization.

"He is now a 15-year-old teenager who has not yet called upon his godfathers for guidance. He has spent two summers in Canada, so the ties that bind us together are strengthened by a new generation."

The princess is shown braving the elements with the Legion's Dominion President Gaston Garceau and attending the ceremony at the cenotaph.

During her West Coast visit, Margriet was introduced to many prominent citizens, including Herman Bergink, then the provincial carillonneur (he has since retired).

For decades, this former Netherlander ascended some eighty-five steps at least twice a week to reach the playing cabin of the handsome carillon tower near the legislative buildings in Victoria. He then proceeded to treat appreciative ears below to a musical offering.

The sixty-two bronze bells, imported from the Netherlands, were a donation of the Dutch-Canadian community of the province in commemoration of Canada's centennial in 1967.

When the carillonneur is not on duty, the bells are activated on the quarter hour by a time clock and a "player piano" roll.

Margriet's mother laid the tower's first stone.

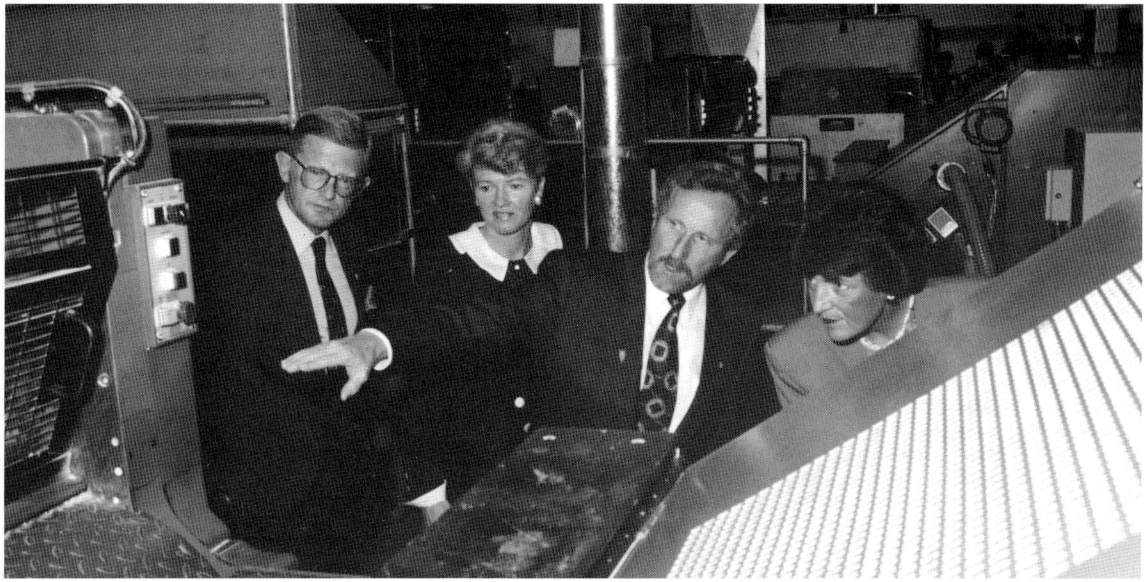

The itinerary also included a tour of the modern printing plant of Hemlock Printers Ltd. in Burnaby, owned and operated by Dick and John Kouwenhoven.

When Dick took over the established business in 1968, there were four employees turning over an annual volume of $85,000 in twelve hundred square feet of space. Since then, the firm has experienced tremendous growth. It now has one hundred and sixty-five employees, does $20 million worth of business a year and operates in a company-owned building of 73,000 square feet.

Margriet showed a keen interest as the various facets of the operations were explained to her. These involved the production of a wide range of subjects, from 150-copy, limited-edition prints to runs of over one million, and from single-color, one-sheet dockets to quality coffee-table books.

Undoubtedly, the princess will return to Canada many more times, to learn first-hand about the success stories of immigrants such as the Kouwenhoven brothers, and to be the guest of honour at various events, all the while reinforcing the close ties that have existed between the land of her birth and the Netherlands since the liberation.

Hundreds of thousands of tulips turn Ottawa into a sea of colour each spring.

They are a vivid reminder of that day in January, 1943, when Canada's princess arrived, when a ray of light suddenly pierced the darkness of war, when everyone was rejuvenated with fresh hopes for triumph and peace.

Canadian Tulip Festival
Festival canadien des tulipes